TRANSFORMATION

_____From a House Girl to a Banker_____

MARY MURIUKI

TRANSFORMATION

ISBN: 978-9966-137-84-5

Po. Box 423-10303
Cell: +254-723-603-739, +254-794-728-035
Wang'uru-Kenya.
Email: marymnjoka2005@gmail.com

Published by
STARLETZ THEATRE & BOOKS
Cell: +254-728-638-801
+254-732-408-689
StarletzTheatre@outlook.com

First published in 2020

Printing and Distribution Physical Address,
Gatakaini Hse/ Lords Hse opp Khoja Mosque
Roundabout, Tom Mboya St, Nairobi-Kenya

DEDICATION

To all the youths in this beloved country and the whole of East Africa with the reassurring message that, "You can make it".

To my beloved parents, the late Mr. Moses Njoka and my darling mother, Phides Njoka who helped greatly in shaping my life.

To my dad and mom in love, Mr. and Mrs. Peter Nyaga who have continually expressed their love to me and treated me as one of their own biological kid.

To my siblings Joseph, Josephat and Joyce, and the entire families of my late dad Mr. Njoka and of Mr. Nyaga.

To my colleagues at work, associates in church who have become a great inspiration in my life.

To my two beloved children Grace and Caleb. Last but importantly, I dedicate this book to my delightful husband, Bernard Muriuki who has really been a great source of strength and encouragement.

ACKNOWLEDGEMENT

It could not have been possible to write this book without the guidance and help of several folks who in one way or another have contributed and extended their valuable assistance.

First, I would like to thank the Almighty God who has answered my prayers and given me strength to pen this book in the face of many obstacles. Thank you, dear Lord.

I would like to appreciate my cherished husband Bernard Muriuki, who has been the source of my strength and encouragement all the time.

Also, I express gratitude to our two lovely children Grace and Caleb who have been our inspiration and a reason for hard work.

I acknowledge my dear brother in Christ and Mentor James M. Kweri, the author of, "BORN A PRINCE LIVED AS A SLAVE". He has walked this journey with me and encouraged my resolve towards this talent.

My brother and long-time friend Churchill, you can't really be forgotten. Your determination to excel by defying all odds has been a great motivation to me.

Special recognition to my valued friend David Kariuki, whom I met in the year 2014 when he was a CEO at Winas Sacco. He has been encouraging me all through and reminding me from time to time that am destined for greatness. Your personal life story is a testimony that we can make it if we keep our spirit alive.

I acknowledge the support of the former education officer Kanyuambora zone Mr. Pius Njiru Kivutu, who kept encouraging me to join college in order to achieve my career goals.

I wish to thank my former boss at Faulu Bank Mr. Raymond Koskey Kibet, a man who made an inerasable difference in my life. Wherever you are, you're truly a commendable great leader. You led and I followed. You stayed close to ensure that I gained every skill I needed to perform my duties well, and you named me a champion. May God bless you.

I also pass my esteems to my supervisors in the working department who kept on encouraging me in this journey and assuring me that I can make it.

Also, I would feel this work is incomplete if I fail to mention Rose Kimani, Henry Ongulo, Edwin Mathu, Kefa Onsongo and Peter Muronchia. I greatly express thanks to the entire Faulu Bank fraternity.
I also recognize my spiritual parents, Bishop Thomas Kigiri of Victory Revival Church- Ngurubani and his wonderful wife who have stood by my family even in the most trying moments.

Finally, I thank the men of God who have kept encouraging me every step of the way. May our good LORD reward you bountifully.

TABLE OF CONTENTS

CHAPTER ONE

Early Life

It was sixteen years after the independence flag was raised when the long journey commenced. In Mbita village, Mbeere South in Embu County, business was not as usual. News spread fast in the entire neighbourhood, and women carrying their baskets could be heard intoning from a far heading to my home.

My household was overwhelmed with bliss like never. It was the first moment to welcome a female child in the family. I remember how my mother told it to me. Holding me in her hands was a flash of satisfaction. Tears welled up in her eyes and she let them stream down her cheeks. She could not leave my sight for a moment. As for my dad and brothers, their faces' glow could never be concealed. One recognized from a far that my household was in jubilation. My father's buddies came along and they patted on his shoulders, shook hands profoundly and giggled.

I was the third child in the family of the late Mr. Moses Njoka, and my beloved mamma's name is Phides Ngithi. I was named after my maternal grandma, hence the name Muthoni. But a single name was not sufficient and a Christian name was to be sought. My mamma with the advice of close relatives settled for Mary, the name of a young virgin lady from Nazareth who became the mother of our saviour Jesus Christ. If by then I had an opportunity to choose, I could have settled for the same. As I grew up, I invariably felt that the Holy Mary was constantly watching over me. After all, we shared a name.

***

My late Papa was among the miraa farming pioneers in the region which subsequently turned to be the essential cash crop in the area. As a result of that, he had exceedingly many friends and people came to him to learn the secret of this magical money-making green leaves. Likewise, he had a substantial lot of consumers, consisting of the then District Officer (D. O), who occasionally used to send his security officers from the nearby police post to get him some.

I recall how a closer view of their guns used to scare us, and in other times, how we used to feel excited and visualized to be like them. Young boys carved wooden guns and excitedly marched around their homes like real police officers either hanging them on their shoulders or holding them as if prepared to terminate an opponent. In other circumstances, people laughed to look at the inexperienced boys in their home gates guarding their homesteads or even using the wooden guns to safeguard the cattle while grazing them in the bushes.

> *He who loves pleasure will*
> *be a poor man; he who loves*
> *wine and oil will not be rich.*
> *~Proverbs 21:17*

The miraa proceeds would have been sufficient to satisfy our elemental needs, and other obligations were it not for my dad's sole religion of drinking. His boundless love for the local brew made him to some degree fail to recall his duties as the head of the family.

It happened that most of his friends also loved the local brew very much. Most of the time, they never came around solely to learn how to grow miraa, but to lure him into spending what he made from the sales. I once remember one of my father's friend who too had a miraa farm, and how the school principal from where his kids schooled enticed him into drinking. The principal consistently showed up whenever the man received his miraa earnings and they went for the local brew until he spent the last coin.

One time it happened that the school fees had accumulated and instead of the principal advising the man to clear the fee balance, they went on drinking as was their routine to the final penny. When the schools opened, the principal sent the kids home to fetch the school fees and it was at this stage when the wife of the man could not stand it any longer. She went to school and confronted the principal for her kids to get back to school. There was no way she could tolerate her kids to stay home, yet the principal was involved in squandering their school fees.

***

I amazingly grew fast because by the fourth month, I supported myself and sat down on my own. This stunned the entire household and especially my mamma who had not witnessed such a thing in the course of bringing up my two brothers. The wonder extended its course in the eighth month when I stood with my two feet.

Unfortunately, towards the end of the year something happened which brought all the happy moments to a halt. I developed a strange illness that made me and mamma to be in and out of the hospital recurrently. The unsurpassed happy little girl in the family, that caused amusement in every individual who came across her became the centre of misfortune. My name turned into a major subject in every prayer said in our household. My mother, who was a Godly trusting woman never gave up. Her faith in God remained irrefutable.

Real disaster struck in 1982 when a terrible famine was experienced in the area. The rain had failed for two consecutive seasons making the region dry and many children and adults lost their lives. The case couldn't have been so severe were it not for the poor farming techniques and poor storage of the produce.

Majority of the children were malnourished and ailments struck them. Families could go for a day or two without a single meal, and sometimes the older sacrificed the scant food they obtained for the young ones. At the time, cassava was the only available diet and at some point, it became troublesome because it caused constipation. Having been sick on a regular basis made me a target of that catastrophe. At some point it became hard for me to eat; I never managed to chew or swallow food and my parents had to liquify it together with fruits in order to save my life. Later,

God's grace took over, and we survived but lost our livestock.

***

Days moved fast, and they turned into months. Months turned into years and within no time, I was old enough to be enrolled in school. I was then admitted to Mbita Primary School, which was three kilometres from home. Thirsty for the white man's knowledge, I met the then nursery school teacher Mrs. Gladys Njue. She was not only enthusiastic in teaching but was also very talented in handling and impacting the white man's knowledge in our little innocent heads. I afterward realized that my siblings also passed through her competent hands.

As for me, learning appeared easy and enjoyable. It consisted of songs, riddles, narratives and numeric counting. The counting of numbers appeared very easy because we recited in unison, turning everything into choruses. That made it simple and similar to the many songs we used to sing.

In narrative, most of the tales were about ogres and other times about the life of an indomitable man born of a virgin from Nazareth. At that time, the story never made sense to us due to our inability to understand things expansively. Later, I came to understand it well enough and I dearly hold and adhere to the teachings to date.

Also, I brightly remember how thrilled I felt when the teacher told us about another man called Moses, who God used to lead His children from the land of bondage- Egypt, to the promised land called Canaan. The teacher told us how God used the man to make a way for His people in the middle of the sea. She also told us how God rained food for them, provided them with water from a rock, gave them ten commandments engraved on two stone tablets and so on and so forth. Everyone yearned to learn more and more and being in school turned out to be a pleasant moment. It turned out that I was also talented in several ways. I used to sing very well that not only did it amaze my family and neighbours, but also teachers and pupils in the entire school. I also did some weaving and modeling.

***

The year was 1993 when I began preparing for the Kenya Certificate of Primary Education (KCPE). The preparations intensified in the last two months as everyone sitting for the exams had his/her dream secondary school to join. During the day, pupils made a lot of consultation from the teachers than it ever occurred before. In the evenings, it was unusual in the villages. Candidates' heads were seen buried in their books revising. Passing the examinations was the major goal of every pupil. Finally, the long-awaited day came, and I did my exams. As I sat for my final paper, I felt certain that I would pass and join high school in the subsequent year.

On 12th December 1993, I gave my live to Christ in a crusade at Mbita ACK grounds. The crusade was organized by Reverend Captain Mary Ngari who is my spiritual mother to date. I greatly cherish her for walking with me in this journey of life and teaching me how to pray and abide in the word of God.

CHAPTER TWO

High School

As anticipated earlier, when the results came out, I had performed exemplary well. I received an admission letter from Kyeni Girls High School offering me a vacancy in form one. Unfortunately, that never materialized because the burden of school fees was becoming unbearable. This was because my elder brothers were also in Secondary school. One was at Kangaru School and the other at Nyangwa Boys High School.

Taking that into consideration, my family opted that I would become the sacrificial lamb. When I realized that I couldn't join the school of my choice that matched so well with my stupendous results, I felt as if nature and business around it were colluding against me. Therefore, I made a vow to myself that in spite of losing a school of my dream, I would never relent.

Subsequently, I had to go to a nearby local boarding school, St. Clare's Kangeta Secondary School. It was 1994 when I commenced secondary school education. At the time, I depicted an impression of a young girl full of power and resolve to learn and silhouette her destiny. I persuaded myself that I still had a space to contest for a brighter tomorrow.

> *It doesn't matter where you are*
> *coming from. All that matters is*
> *where you are going.*
> *~Brian Tracy*

Going to High School accelerated my willpower, and I remained sharp in both curricular and co-curricular tasks. I adored Biology subject so much that it was my all-time ticket to the Science Congress Competitions.

Correspondingly, I truly shined in poetry, athletic and I was a Christian Union leader.

One of the main challenges was waking up at dawn to prepare for the class. Waking up late meant that matters would take a wrong turn because no one would flee the wrath of the teacher on duty. Another challenge for me was bathing with ice-cold water. Just like many of other students, it caused chills on me. Nevertheless, I knew remarkably well that completing High School was more important than any of that. On the other hand, our day commenced with devotional prayers at 3:00AM. This strengthened our spirit in God and we felt peaceful to cast our burdens on Him.

***

After spending two years at St. Clare's Kangeta Secondary School, I was transferred to St. Agnes Girls- Kiaganari. The most regrettable part about it was that they made me repeat form two owing to lack of a vacancy in form three. I never complained much.

> *Throughout our lives we are faced*
> *with a variety of challenges. It is in*
> *these moments that the wisdom of*
> *others who have walked the same*
> *dark valleys but have overcome*
> *prove to be invaluable and*
> *sometimes the catalyst for*
> *our own personal triumphs*
> *and victories.*
> *~Rusell and Sam Evans*

In the meantime, I looked at it as a better chance to excel in my studies now that the school was pretty and accommodating.

The new 'pretty' school as I described it also came with its anguishes. I was in and out of school recurrently than before due to school fees arrears. The worst part of it was a third term in form three where

I spent the entire term away from school. An incidence that made me miss my mock examination, which was used to figure out who was qualifying for the next class- form four.

By God's grace, early the following year something cropped up. One of the Board members discovered that my name was missing in the end-of-year exam Merit List. This was mainly because I was one of the surpassingly performing student and therefore, my absence from the Merit List was a gap that was easily detected.

During the school's Board of Governors meeting, they raised the question about my absence in the Merit List. The school Principal explained to the Board what had taken place. When the Board understood that I was away due to lack of school fees, it was resolved there and then that I was to be called back to go on with the studies. What ensued was that the Board footed all the outstanding fees. On receiving the marvelous news, I immediately reported back with appreciativeness. Regardless of the fact that I never did my end of the year exam, I was endorsed to the next class. Every time I was sent home, my biggest role was to dig in people's farms and save the little pay I got for the school fees. I also spent a lot of time in prayers and fasting and God always came to my rescue.

CHAPTER THREE

Unbearable Loss

In the same year in February, my world came tumbling after losing my dad. He capitulated to death after a short illness. Giving up never occurred in my dad's terminology. For him, a stomachache or a cough was just an inconsequential thing to notice. Therefore, it never passed over my mind that his demise would be so sudden.

> *Remember that in difficult times,*
> *we don't give up. We don't*
> *discard our highest ideals. No!*
> *We rise up to meet them.*
> *~Michelle Obama*

The burial arrangements commenced and after a few days, we laid him to rest. It took us quite some time to come into terms with his sudden departure. It's presumed that it's natural for girls to be more connected to their fathers. That's why it became particularly complicated for me to be in tranquility for a long time.

During the grief-stricken time, my younger sister was left behind the shadows. Nobody took notice of her yet she was supposed to join the secondary school at around that time. Having sat for her class eight examinations the preceding year, it was just by bad luck that the unfortunate set of circumstances overlapped her preparations of joining high school.

I feared for her situation when I realized how troubled and depressed, she was. From the look of things, one could tell that she was experiencing a convoluted time than anyone else in the family. I feared that she would never get a chance to go to a secondary school. Then, it was my duty as an elder sister to be audacious in order to comfort and give hope to her. In the face of what had transpired, life had to continue, and we had to face the reality of things.

***

There comes a time when you have to forget about yourself and regard the Wants and well-being of others.

The minute my brothers completed high school, they came back home and proceeded to work on the family's miraa farm. By doing so, my younger sister managed to be enrolled to school. During that time, I found myself preparing for the examinations at the culmination of the year. There was no time to waste and I had to stick to designed moves if at all I desired to pass the exams.

On the other hand, we formed a prayer team with some of my dearest colleagues, where we pledged to carry on with the task even after accomplishing our final examinations. We planned where and when we would meet to go for missions, pray and visit the old and the sick. We sincerely felt an urge to give back to the society, and also serve God. The idea of where I had come from, and where I projected to get stirred my lifeforce and made me work even harder than before. Time seemed to elapse fast and within no time, I sat for my exams.

***

Freedom was at the helm as I felt that I was now a grown up. Having successfully completed the high school course wasn't an inconsequential achievement, bearing in mind the many impediments I had bumped into along the way. Everyone in the neighbourhood had assumed I would give up, but later on, they were the same people extolling me for the perseverance.

For the time being, I kept myself busy with farm work which was easier to find in the villages. It was December and crops were plentiful and labour work was invariably in high demand at that period. I was an expert when it came to farm work. I had gained the skills with time because whenever we closed the school; I spent the better part of my time at the farms. This was either in my home or in the neighbourhood.

Finally, the long-waited results were out. I had not performed very well as people had hoped, but I believed that I had done temporarily well. Bearing in mind the time I had spent home now and then because of school fees issues, I felt that I had made an exceptional shot.

I received an admission letter to join Kenya Medical Training College (KMTC), to train as a nurse. I felt that the Lord was on my side, and that He had answered my ever prayers. This was because, I had aspired to be a nurse. If not that, a pastor or a police officer. I hoped to give service to people.

> *Sometimes when you sacrifice something precious, you are not really losing it. You are just passing it on to someone else.*
> *~Mitch Albom*

Unfortunately, as fate dictated it, I could not join the Medical College for the evident reasons- lack of tuition fees. My younger sister's educational needs were of a larger priority than everything else. All that made sense to me because I knew that she needed an opportunity to learn too. There was no way I could have let her sacrifice her secondary school education so that I could go to college. I genuinely believed that she deserved a chance too, and I believed that she would make good use of it. Therefore, she continued with her studies, and I kept doing what I had already attained dexterity on- farming.

CHAPTER FOUR

The Hustle

After what looked like an introduction into the 'real world', I had to move out and try to make the ends meet. After a hunt, I secured a house girl job at a place called Ishiara- Embu. It was a home of a certain schoolteacher in the area. My salary was Kshs. 700 per month. At that time, the wage appeared just fine for I had no other choice.

My working hours commenced at 5.00AM. On waking up, I had to prepare the family's breakfast and get the children ready for school. The two kids were in the lower primary school and to some length, that made my work easier. After ensuring that all was in place, I then took the kids to school and once back, I cleaned the house, washed and ironed the clothes.

In the evening, I went for the children from school, assisted them in doing their homework, bathed them and ensured that they took their supper on time. They were required to go to bed early. After the owners of the house had taken their meals to gratification, I then prepared for the next day by washing the utensils and putting everything else in order.

There was a TV set in the house which my employers never allowed me to set eyes on. I thus could never tell it aired what type of the programs. I simply heard them talking of how great a certain TV show was and how they enjoyed every second spent watching it. They made sure that I heard the compliments they made about those programs. Also, I could not set my foot in the living room unless when tidying the place, or when they needed me to do something that called for my presence there.

*Opportunities to find deeper powers
within ourselves come when life
seems most challenging.
~Joseph Campbell*

Another thing I experienced that appeared quite humiliating was that, there were some type of food I was not allowed to serve. For instance, whenever we cooked meat, chapati or rice, the mother of the house made sure that she served the meals herself. As if that was not enough, she marked the level of food in the cooking pot to ensure that I would not touch it. That was after ensuring that she served me as little as possible. However, I handled everything gracefully knowing very well that challenges were not meant to break me, but to make me stronger.

I recall that one day after I received my pay, together with some savings I had, I took the children to the market to do some shopping. I bought gifts for them and then realized that there was no way I would go back to the house without a basket of fruits. This was because, since the first day I stepped in that home, I was never authorized to eat the fruits. They were solely meant for the members of that house.

When the mother of the house came back and realized that I had taken the kids out, bought them gifts, did some shopping that included a whole basket of fruits of various kinds, it amazed her. It was then after that day when I realized that she had changed. She began treating me a little well.

Now that I could not mingle with the family in the sitting room, I used to spend most of my time in the kitchen and that's where I used to take my meals from or in my bedroom. My evening duties came to an end between 9:30-10:00PM. Therefore, since I had my personal things to work on, which sometimes included reading a novel or doing some Bible studies, I ended up retiring to bed at 11:00PM.

Apart from the house help job, I was also a Sunday school teacher in the local Full Gospel Churches of Kenya. The church was a few miles away. Therefore, I made sure that my work schedule was well defined to avoid disrupting my church obligations.

***

After working for six months, I landed on what I could term as a greener pasture. It was the same job description with a salary increment of Kshs. 100. I felt joyous and satisfied. Less did I know that I had jumped from the flying pan to the fire. When I got there, the new boss assigned to me more responsibilities which included milking the cows, taking the milk to the dairy and tilling the garden.

Those extra duties were beyond my capacities. I did the job for one month and then gave up. I opted to return to my former employer who took me in without a query. She loved my dexterity and fortitude towards work.

*Perseverance is the hard work you do
after you get tired of doing the hard
work you already did.
~Newt Gingrich*

CHAPTER FIVE

The Photographer

I met a schoolteacher by the name Mr. Mwangi, who taught at Karangare Secondary School to date. He opened a photo studio in Ishiara market and placed me in charge. The name of the studio was 'A TO Z COMPLEX'. I now had two jobs: a photographer and a house help. Balancing the two was not a simple task, it meant more sweat.

To begin with, I had to wake up at 4:00AM, wash clothes, prepare the children for school by 7:00AM, and open the studio at 8:00AM. My main clients at the studio were students and pupils from the nearby schools, St. Monica Girls Secondary School, St. Peter's Boarding Primary School and the public. At last, I saw my salary rise to Kshs. 3000 which was far much better than what I was earning. So, by all means I felt I was at the right place.

At 4:00PM, I had to pick the kids from school and take them home. Then I returned to the studio and worked for one more hour. On getting home in the evening, I prepared supper and as usual assisted the kids in doing their homework. By the time I completed my day's errands, I used to be so tired such that I succumbed to sleep without a warning. Sometimes I ended up sleeping on the chair in the kitchen.

After I tried my best to balance on the two jobs for a month, I dropped the house help job after getting them a satisfying replacement. The later house help was a wonderful friend of mine and they welcomed her without a question, now that they had grown to trust me. Since then, I turned into a full-time photographer.

When I wasn't very busy at the studio, I took some painting jobs around to make a few more coins. The idea about the painting jobs was induced to me by Mr. Mwangi. He more than once re-counted to me his achievement story, and how he transformed every challenge and problem he came across into a stepping stone. His stories kept inspiring me to become more and do better.

Whenever I wore the untidy blue-black overall during the painting time, I looked 'professional'. The comments from those I came across gave me confidence in that field which, until then, I knew very little about. I also became a motivation to very many youngsters within that locality. By observing what I did, they honestly affirmed that anyone can become anything.

> *He who would learn to fly one day*
> *must first learn to stand and walk*
> *and run and climb and dance; one*
> *cannot fly into flying.*
> *~Nietzsche*

***

In January 2001, I searched for a greener pasture and travelled to Nyahururu. While there, I got a teaching job in a private high school at a place called Kasuku. I taught Physics and Chemistry and I never liked the profession. Teaching was far from my dreams. After working for two terms I contemplated quitting the job, and move on to something I was okay with. More to that, the wage was on no occasion proportionate to the work done.

After leaving the teaching job, I decided to try beauty therapy and hairdressing. I got a job in a salon where I was paid on commission. Life became tough since customers were not frequent as I had anticipated or would have wanted it to be. It got to a point where I couldn't hang on it any longer but to think of a "Plan B".

I stuck for two months at the salon which seemed like an eternity and fortunately, I got a job in an Agro Vet. The job entailed selling Agro Chemicals and animal feeds to the farmers. The owner also required me to make occasional visits to their homes to check on their livestock. After some time, I felt that the job was not satisfying my expectations. Therefore, after working for three months, I left. While there, I learned some basic veterinary principles which I apply to date.

***

Luck was again on my side and it never took me long to get another job. I got a secretarial job at a company called JAPENDA ENTREPRISES. The firm dealt with second-hand vehicles as well as buying and selling plots. It was during this time after seeing how things were running in the business, when a thought of going to college crossed my mind. I sustained the feelings and with no time, the idea had obsessed my mind. Whether asleep or awake, I dreamt about going to college. Sincerely, everything whirled around it.

My plans came to practicality the following year. After ensuring that all was set, I enrolled for a certificate in secretarial course. That took place at RWIKA TECHNICAL INSTITUTE, the subsequent JEREMIAH NYAGA TECHNICAL INSTITUTE. I had saved enough money to cater for my tuition fees. The course took one and half years. Time flew quicker than I had supposed and before contemplating it, I was through with my course. It was then that I resolved to try my luck in the capital city- Nairobi.

> *You don't get lucky while sitting on*
> *the sofa with arms crossed doing*
> *nothing. You can be lucky only when*
> *you are prepared.*
> *~Nesta Jojoe Erskine*

CHAPTER SIX

The Real Setback

That day, left home full of optimism and determination to succeed. The real disaster struck a few minutes upon the arrival in the capital city. I had not predicted that the city had transformed so much from my early visits. There were new buildings, bus stops appeared modernized, and the streets were jammed with people. It seemed that every day in Nairobi meant more people visiting and occupying the area.

Hawkers were heard singing their charming melodies of how cheap and durable their commodities were. The matatu conductors were busy touting and everyone appeared busy on their business. I witnessed a situation where a young lady was carried shoulder high to the bus by the bus conductor because she had taken too long to decide which bus to board. Some members of the public including me stared at the scene stunned, while others laughed. By the look of things, I felt as if I was visiting Nairobi for the first time.

I tried to maneuver my way to the Industrial Area. Moving around the downtown, I tried to recall which route to take. At some point I felt tempted to ask for the directions, but I feared that someone might deceive me and steal my things. My bag that practically had everything that I owned hang on my back. I slowly found myself at Haile Selassie Avenue. There, I met some rioting students whom I later came to learn that they were from Nairobi Polytechnic, the consequent, Technical University of Kenya.

Amid the chaos, students threw stones and anything else their hands could get hold of to the police officers. The officers tried to handle the situation and retaliated by firing tears gas. That seemed to me like tiny smoky grenades. Everyone ran helter-skelter to save themselves from the gas.

I found myself entangled in the group of students and I couldn't tell where I was not to mention my bag. Later, the acrimonious truth dawned to me, I had lost it. It contained my important documents like original academic certificates and the national identification card. Left with nothing apart from the dress I was wearing, and several coinages in my pocket that amounted to ten shillings, I coiled at the side of the street shuddering in shock.

You have not lived today until you have
done something for someone who can
never repay you.
~John Bunyan

A kind matatu driver noticed my state of confusion from afar. He walked to me and after we exchanged greetings, I narrated to him what had befallen me and he assisted me to locate my way to Lungalunga. I thank God for the man's kindness was genuine, and he never thought of taking advantage of me. A cousin of mine took me in and offered me a house help job.

I realized that life in the city meant I had no other better option than to start afresh. I applied for a new identity card and began a long journey of recuperation from what had taken place. That incident has remained as an unforgettable nightmare to me up to the present time.

***

After a short while, I moved out and jointly with a friend we rented a simple house in Sinai, Lungalunga. The rental was Kshs. 600, and we struggled a lot to raise the cash. Most of the times, the rent consumed almost everything that we made. I worked here and there without a particular job I could identify myself with.

All the time, I woke up early in the morning and wandered around expecting to find something valuable to do. I searched for a job for a relatively lengthy time and I realized that looking for a job had become my new job. Later, I found myself in a Darling Company in Industrial Area which dealt with human hair. The work entailed packaging the hair and wages were on a weekly basis.

Life became tough and at some point, I turned into a hawker. Some commodities I vended were air freshener, socks, pens, handkerchiefs among many other things. The traffic jams along Jogoo Road and other areas used to favour my petite business. That was because, those stuck in the traffic flow became my most important customers. However, it never went far because of the hostility and constant harassment by the county council police.

One day, the youths from the church I used to attend bought a dress for me. It was after they saw that I only had one that I used to wear on all occasions. Later on, I got a job with Pharm Chem Pharmaceutical. They paid me after a fortnight which was an answered prayer for me because life was hard.

***

After a while, I moved from Sinai to Mukuru kwa Njenga, and later to Tassia Estate. While there, I got a secretarial job and also became an assistant pastor in one church. I will never forget Bishop Titus and Rev. Agnes Masika who took me as their own daughter, and they nurtured me to what I am today. Among other roles that I played in the church were ensuring that the order of the service was observed, discipleship classes were attended, winning souls to Christ and organizing for crusades. Later, I was employed as a merchandiser by a sanitary towels manufacturing company in Kirinyaga Road, where I worked for 6 months.

CHAPTER SEVEN

A Wedding of my Dream

While in college, I fell in love with a gracious young gentleman, Mr. Bernard Muriuki. We courted and discussed our wedding plans. By the grace of God, on 17th December 2005, we walked down the aisle and exchanged our marriage vows at Full Gospel Churches of Kenya (FGCK) in Kithimu, Embu. This was after five years of courtship.

My life transformed completely because I had someone I could confide to whenever I encountered a complicated task. I cherish this gentleman (the love of my life), for the way he took me and regarded me with devotion and care. He kept encouraging and training me on how to grow into an excellent prayer warrior and serve God. To date, he has remained my greatest companion. If someone would ask me to go back in time and choose, I would definitely fall for him over and over endlessly.

*Pray in your family daily, that yours
may be in the number of the families
who call upon God.
~Christopher Love*

The Lord has graciously blessed us with two children, Grace and Caleb who have invariably become our best source of joy. Grace is now 12 years old, and she is developing into a marvelous minister of the word of God and we exalt the Lord for that. Our son Caleb, just like the great man who remained strong in his eighties according to the Bible, is a great singer who always nourishes our spirit every time we are together as a family.

***

Now, some years after our wedding, we saved some money that could help us start a family business. This was after a thorough discussion about it. As soon as we finalized all the arrangements, I resigned from the company I was working for and started a family business. I sold *vitenge*, handbags and shoes. I sourced them from as far as Tanzania, Uganda and Congo.

The business prettied, and we felt that it was getting us to a remarkable level. Therefore, I felt inclined to work harder because I smelled success. I felt I had already encountered enough troubles to enable me discern what could work and what could not. I knew precisely that any business venture was a speculative risk, and I was willing to face mine.

Issues started later when I was diagnosed with stomach ulcers. I later learned that it was as a result of excessive consumption of *Sukuma wiki*. That was not a surprise to me because it was our main diet, and as it went with lower- and middle-class populaces of Nairobi. I thank God the problem was diagnosed on time and the doctor applied the right methods of treatment.

Our thriving business was brought to an abrupt end by the 2007/2008 post-election violence. At that time, our firstborn child (Grace) was only seven months old, and we were living in Pipeline Estates. One day while in my usual line of duty at Dohnholm, a vehicle was set ablaze as I watched. Then the entire surrounding area became turbulent due to political tension. Several customers were killed on the spot, businesses ransacked and some customers vanished with unpaid items. This trend of things went on for a long time and before things normalized, a number of small and medium businesses had closed down including mine.

CHAPTER EIGHT

The New Dawn

*Those who wait upon the lord will
never be disappointed.
~Isaiah 40.28-31*

After countless prayers and patience, the Lord opened a door for me. It was on 3rd February 2008, when a friend told me to take my application to Faulu Microfinance Ltd, the later Faulu Bank. When I took my application letter, I found a gentle man by the name Earnest Mbitha. Mr. Earnest took time and talked to me because I appeared very desperate.

Later, I learned that he was a born-again Christian who feared the Lord. He ensured that I met with his boss, a lady by the name Hellen Osore, whom I later grew to like for her benevolence. During the job interview, she asked me the salary expectation per month, and I swiftly answered ten thousand Kenya shillings.

First, that sounded like a lot of money to me. Second, I feared that mentioning a huge amount would result to the loss of that opportunity. She then told me that if I got the job, it would be a matter of time and a salary of ten thousand would never again reverberate in my mind.

Heartily, I praised God and beseeched Him to teach me patience and grant me a passion for that work. I painfully remembered how my household lost a business that produced a substantial amount of money. Therefore, after a lengthy talk I accepted the offer. They then enrolled me as a housekeeper along with the customer care officer. The post was on a casual basis where they paid me kshs.200 per day worked.

I devoted myself zealously to what they assigned me to do. Within the first year, I recruited over four thousand customers. After a while, they transferred me to the main branch at OTC to work as a customer care officer. My predecessor there was promoted to a branch manager and transferred to Thika branch. My working terms improved, and I moved from a casual employee to working under a contract which led to salary increment.

In August 2009, I did an interview in the same institution and they confirmed me as a permanent staff early 2010. In the same year, they transferred me to Mwea branch. My industrious nature kept on shining because the Lord's grace was upon me. Within one year of service in Mwea, together with other members of the staff, we recruited a sizeable number of customers and raised a loan book of over 400 million. Within no time, they promoted me to sales team leader. Mwea branch was quite extensive as it also composed of Kerugoya and Embu areas.

After a long period of hard work, we caught the eye of the management and as a result; we became a benchmark for others, and we were ranked third in the whole country. Around mid-2014, our branch manager resigned, and they appointed me as the interim branch manager. I held the position for almost a year. As time went by, my managerial skills sharpened even more. Every day, I loved the manager I had become.

I wasn't made to remain in Mwea branch forever and in the fifth month of 2015; they transferred me to execute my duties in Embu branch. I fully embraced the transfer because it brought me closer to my roots. However, my stay in Embu was not much eventful and was also short-lived. With the comfort and notion of being at home, relaxed with nothing much to worry about, I moved out of Faulu Bank.

THE END

Dear Reader,

I trust you have enjoyed perusing my story. I feel grateful that I had to share it, to motivate and help you examine and determine what you want to become in this precious life God has given to us. In my next book, I will unfold what happened after I resigned from Faulu Bank and what I am up to. Thank you so much for reading, **TRANSFORMATION**.